Managing High-Maintenance Employees

by

Lin O'Neill

Bloomington, IN   Milton Keynes, UK

authorHOUSE®

AuthorHouse™
1663 Liberty Drive, Suite 200
Bloomington, IN 47403
www.authorhouse.com
Phone: 1-800-839-8640

AuthorHouse™ UK Ltd.
500 Avebury Boulevard
Central Milton Keynes, MK9 2BE
www.authorhouse.co.uk
Phone: 08001974150

First published by AuthorHouse 4/10/2007

ISBN: 978-1-4343-0882-5 (sc)

Library of Congress Control Number: 2007902724

Printed in the United States of America
Bloomington, Indiana

This book is printed on acid-free paper.

The Simple Series is written for busy people wrestling with important supervisory, management and leadership topics in today's organizations. The author's goal is to provide easy to implement solutions for issues affecting productivity and profitability in today's workplace.

Dedication:
To RHS, MK, RL, TM and TAW, superior Mentors all.

Contents

INTRODUCTION

I'm actually not sure just when my interest in high-maintenance employees surfaced. I suspect, though, it had to do with someone giving me some rather direct feedback. Yes, I confess. At a couple of points in my career, I have been a High Maintenance Employee. I've also hired, fired (and successfully coached) folks just like me.

When I've wondered how I came to be high-maintenance, I've found there are several fertile fields in my background in which the high-maintenance seeds could have flowered.

The important fact is that *it doesn't matter*... for me, for you, for employers, co-workers or employees. Discovering how we arrived at the adoption of this persona isn't the primary issue... resolving its impact effectively...that is.

When considering high-maintenance corrective approaches, two truths are very important:

1. Most high-maintenance employees want to do a good (maybe even great) job

   and

2. High-maintenance behavior is incredibly costly.

These are the aspects of high-maintenance with which we'll deal in this little book.

THE CHALLENGE

High-maintenance employees are a "soft dollar" direct hit to the bottom line of your organization. Whether your business is large, medium or small--in the public or private sector--you will profit from the information offered in this brief look at one of the:

- most misunderstood workplace challenges
- most costly operational issues of the modern workplace
  and
- one of the greatest organizational opportunities available to accelerate both productivity and profitability.

I've already made reference to the fact that most high-maintenance employees want to do a good job. In other words, high-maintenance employees don't sit with their morning cup of coffee or tea and say to themselves, "I think I'll be high-maintenance today." High-maintenance behaviors are learned as coping mechanisms and become habits, ways to get needs met in a situation or environment where it feels as though that isn't likely to happen.

> *NOTE: Often the high-maintenance person's needs aren't going to be met because what he or she really wants is someone to be straight with them and they've placed themselves in an issue-avoiding organizational culture. When this occurs, the high-maintenance person's high-maintenance behavior is likely to get exponentially more outrageous until those affected finally confront, defining boundaries for which the high-maintenance individual has been searching. Once confronted, the high-maintenance person will make a decision to change or leave.*
>
> *NOTE: If the organization has been relying on the high-maintenance person for its drama factor, it may be slower to confront, being loathe to give up the entertainment.*

In many organizations, high-maintenance employee behaviors result from poor, misguided or absent recognition systems. Over and over again I've seen, when there's no readily apparent way to gain positive attention in the workplace, an otherwise productive employee may take charge of getting her or his own attention through high-maintenance actions.

A client once retained my services to assist in resolving a series of conflicted [high-maintenance] situations. After the first few conflicts were resolved, it was clear the conflicts [high-maintenance behaviors] were being used as a backdrop to showcase previously-shot-down suggested actions for specific departments or the organization as a whole. We, my Client and I, set about formalizing a "positive change" *[suggestion]* process and the conflicts [high-maintenance behaviors] stopped almost immediately.

It's also important to note that high-maintenance employees appear at all levels in our organizations. It's not at all uncommon to find a high-maintenance Chairman, President, CEO or Executive Director.

One example from my personal experience was a president who, in the midst of an organization's greatest crisis…became obsessed with spots on a carpet. Seriously! When his direct reports would have—much more effectively—been laying out competitive strategy, they were rounding up people to spot clean a bit of rug. I'm not saying clean rugs weren't important…they just paled by comparison with the other organizational challenges faced at that time.

The president's high-maintenance behavior cost the organization, literally and figuratively.

As in that example, the impact of high-maintenance behavior cannot be evaluated in a vacuum. High-maintenance employees' behavior has a measurable effect on the attitudes, focus and satisfaction, as well as the productivity, of those with whom they come in contact (or who hear about them from others).

So…who are high-maintenance employees?

- *Employees who prompt you to sigh when you see them heading your way*
- *Employees who require special levels of attention and time*
- *Employees who want to debate every assignment or instruction*
- *Employees who blame to excuse their mis-steps*
- *Employees who consistently fail to meet established objectives*
- *Employees who don't perform…and are politically linked to someone above you in the organization*
- *Employees who are living on their previous reputation and not performing acceptably today*

In other words, high-maintenance employees encourage you to spend more time, more money and more energy than specific situations would require if they were being addressed in a productive and effective manner.

Often high-maintenance employees just wear you down. When faced with the dilemma of the high maintenance employee, many managers just give in or hide out. Neither approach is effective.

And if you've bought into the less-than-productive theory that an open door policy means you must be accessible every minute of every day, you have the proverbial bull's-eye on your back as far as the high-maintenance employee is concerned.

It is my experience—so of course I believe it is true—that the antidote for High-Maintenance-it is is what I call a capitalist's discussion, in which high-maintenance actions are linked to dollar amounts. But, I'm getting ahead of myself...that is covered in the sections on "The Cure" and "Sample Scripts."

Employees who prompt you to sigh when you see them heading your way

We've all been there…you look down the hall, see a certain employee headed your way and your flight instinct is activated. Why? Because you know the now seemingly unavoidable conversation is going to play havoc with your plans for a productive day.

Employees who require special levels of attention and time

In every supervisory and managerial training class I attended during the formative years of my career, it seems to me there was universal agreement about the importance of being available to employees. After all, this was the height of the "open door policy" thinking.

Well, I do believe in availability and open doors... when there is an appointment, a sincere need or a crisis. I also believe in the right to close your door when you're in a crunch or need thought time. That's why doctors and dentists have office hours. The key, of course, is to explain your philosophy to those with and for whom you work and who work with and for you.

Without a full commitment to productivity, a continually open door can be an invitation to waste... of time, energy and money.

Employees who want to debate every assignment or instruction

This version of high-maintenance employee costs time and money in two ways...one obvious, one sometimes less so:

Extra time is used to convince the employee about what is to be done (i.e., the desirable end result).

Extra time is also used when significant additional time is spent explaining and/or writing out assignments in an effort to avoid the dreaded debates.

And...as the saying goes, time is money!

Employees who blame others for their mis-steps

The extra cost to an organization in this situation is either the investigative time or the counseling time as you work to supplement what is probably a lack of accountability training in childhood.

I remember my sweet little Aunt Maurine saying, "It's not about your cousins and what they did. It's about you and what you did." Ah...words of wisdom! And a good model in the workplace, too.

Employees who consistently fail to meet established objectives

The first question here, of course, is: Does the employee have the skills to perform the work. If not, rather than being a typical incidence of high-maintenance, it may be a genuine cry for help with training as the appropriate step.

The operative word here is <u>consistently</u>. If the employee has the skills and still isn't performing, in spite of your assistance, this employee may need to move to another position, another organization, and/or another planet.

Employees who don't perform...but are politically linked to someone above you in the organization

This is always fun since your corrective efforts may knowingly, or unknowingly, be thwarted. If you know the high-maintenance employee's guardian angel, a diplomatic conversation over a cup of coffee might work, giving you an ally in the high-maintenance change process.

If you don't know this person, or your direct contact isn't going to be looked upon favorably, you may want to invoke the 6° of separation theory and find a trusted resource to help.

A third strategy is to have an initial conversation with the high-maintenance employee in question (just as you would with any high-maintenance employee) and sit back because your conversation is likely to flush out the sponsor.

In this situation, tread softly. You can accomplish the high-maintenance change you want and need, just pay attention to the power structure.

Employees who are living on their previous reputation and not performing acceptably today

These high-maintenance employees spend interminable hours rehashing past situations and their glorious role in resolution.

Also, their blocking of new and creative ideas results in others having to spend significantly more time to win approval for their concepts and approaches over this high-maintenance person's war story models.

What "makes" Employees high maintenance?

There are, no doubt, a number of reasons and four of the most prevalent are shown below.

1. "Wrong" position
2. No connection to Vision/Mission
3. Ineffective recognition systems
4. Negative attention is better than no attention

"Wrong" position

Innumerable studies have been done about the ways people end up in their jobs and careers. The most common response when asked about this is, "I just kinda fell into it."

"Just falling" often leads to dissatisfaction and dissatisfaction often leads to high-maintenance behaviors like constant approval seeking, expressed and requested affirmations of importance and conflict encouragement.

No connection to the Vision/Mission

Purpose and energy are inextricably linked. When an individual "buys in" to the Vision/Mission, their energy rises, focus becomes sharp and positive forward movement is increased.

With the absence of any of these clues, it's a good bet that an open and honest Vision/ Mission discussion would be a good next step. Without it, the productivity potential of the detached employee may crater and high-maintenance behavior take its place...a double cost whammy for the organization.

Ineffective recognition systems

Recognition is the term we tend to use for "business love."

One of my greatest mentors once told me that, "All fully-functioning humans want to be loved and wanted." I believe he was right.

This makes the presence of an *effective* recognition system paramount in every organization.

I hope you noted that I italicized and underlined the word "effective." This emphasis is based on the unbelievable number of "recognition systems" I've seen put in place—often at GREAT expense—that just don't get the job done. Most often this is because someone somewhere made a decision about what employees want and/or how to give it to them, forgetting that "humans buy into that which we help create."

The best example of this in my career was when I worked for a highly profitable division of a Fortune 100 company. We had money to burn and wanted to use the fire to inspire and recognize our employees. The methodology chosen was a 4-color glossy publication that was absolutely beautiful! In fact, it won a number of prestigious awards. The problem we encountered was the high-maintenance behavior of employees boy-cotting the publication and many requests for the information that was previously included in com-pany publications. The employee group wanted to know about service anniversaries, who just had a baby, who had been promoted and similar bits of news. We finally got smart and printed up what the employees wanted. Guess what? The high-maintenance behaviors disappeared. We could hardly print them fast enough. Everyone read them and they turned out to be a great com-munication vehicle for our Vision and Mission.

It was hard to give up the pretty pictures…and we had to re-examine our goal: effective communi-cation and buy-in.

Negative attention is better than no attention

I mentioned this earlier and the topic is closely tied to the previous one except this one is, probably, more personal. The high-maintenance behavior that results from lack of attention tends to play out most often in one-on-one and team interactions.

An illustration that most of us have experienced or observed comes from family life...picture this scenario:

A parent comes home from a long and challenging day on the job. He or she wants time to sit in a favorite chair, sip a glass of wine and read the paper or watch the evening news on television.

Having just settled in, the parent is approached by a child who wants to talk, ask a question, explain something that happened at daycare or school.

The parent, craving some time to recalibrate, says to the child, "Sweetheart, just give Mom (or Dad) 15 minutes and then we'll _____ [...talk, read a book, play catch...]. You fill in the blank.

Now the child may not have mastered time telling...and you can bet he or she will be back in... exactly 15 minutes. When re-approached, Dad (or Mom) may beg for "...just 5 more minutes." And the child may acquiesce.

However, if this continues for very long, isn't it true that the child will have a tantrum, start an argument with siblings, pull the dog's tail or break something. Why? You've got it: Negative attention is better than no attention.

This need, on our parts, is large...and, as adults in the workplace, we're just kids in bigger bodies. Many high-maintenance employees are just wanting sincere attention.

THE CURE

The "cure" for high-maintenance behaviors in the workplace revolves around explaining their organizational cost.

As mentioned a couple of times, most employees want to do a good job and, if advised that they are not (that is, they are costing their employer unnecessarily in time and money expended) most will change their ways.

The first step in preparation for the "high-maintenance discussion" is calculating the individual's compensation, down to the minute, or—if you prefer—down to the second.

You can effectively use the individual's

- salary
- salary + bonus
- salary + bonus + benefits

…you get the idea. The important thing is, when you have the "high maintenance discussion," to clarify the compensation formula you are using.

MEDICAL CENTER

NAME _____ AGE _____
ADDRESS _____ DATE _____

R⅄

_____

SIGNATURE

□ LABEL

REFILL 0 1 2 3 4 5 PRN NR

It is also important, when preparing for the "High-Maintenance Discussion," to do a physical/mental/emotional check.

	√
Physical:	
• Is my selected location discussion-friendly	
○ We won't be disturbed	
○ The desk barrier is eliminated	
○ The colors I'm wearing are conducive to trust, intelligence, openness	
○ My body language tendencies have been reviewed and adjusted as appropriate	
Mental:	
• My mindset is positive	
Emotional:	
• I am feeling calm and open	

What do High-Maintenance Employees cost?

ANNUAL SALARY	HOURLY RATE	MINUTE RATE	5-minute high-maintenance conversation cost	15-minute high-maintenance conversation cost
$20,000.00	$9.62	$0.16	$0.80	$2.40
$40,000.00	$19.23	$0.32	$1.60	$4.81
$60,000.00	$28.85	$0.48	$2.40	$7.21
$80,000.00	$38.46	$0.64	$3.21	$9.62
$100,000.00	$48.08	$0.80	$4.01	$12.02

Well…that doesn't look too bad.

What happens if you annualize this cost?

		Weekly Cost	Individual Annual Cost	Total Annual Cost
Two :15 "High-Maintenance" conversations per week	Employee	$4.81	$240.38	
($20,000 per year Employee with $60,000 per year Supervisor):	Supervisor	$14.42	$721.15	$961.54
**assuming 2 weeks' vacation*				
Two :15 "High-Maintenance" conversations per week	Employee	$19.23	$923.08	
($80,000 per year Employee with $100,000 per year Supervisor):	Supervisor	$24.04	$1,153.85	$2,076.92
**assuming 4 weeks' vacation*				

Still not unbearable...

And if that one $60,000 a year Supervisor has 2 fifteen-minute high-maintenance conversations with three $20,000 per year employees each week?

The annual cost to the organization jumps up to $2,884.62.

And what if one of your $100K per year executives has 2 fifteen-minute high-maintenance conversations with one of his or her $100k per year peers each week?

That cost is $2,307.69 annually.

Now, to me (as a small business owner these days), these numbers are outrageous. And truthfully, in the grand scheme of things, they're not going to break the bank for many companies. On the other hand, let's say you have, out of your 50,000 employees, 15 executives who have 2 fifteen-minute high-maintenance conversations with one of their peers each week (except when they're on vacation).

That cost is roughly $35,000.00 or, said another way, those high-maintenance conversations cost you the price of an administrative assistant for one of your departments that has been begging Human Resources to process a requisition for a person to answer their phones.

The sad truth is that, in most organizations, there are many more minutes, and hours, *[read: $$$$]* being spent in high-maintenance activities than most of us would believe.

I want to clarify here that I am not in favor of an organization where there are no casual conversations, pleasantries or fun. In fact, the opposite is true. Some of the most creative experiences I've had in organizations have started out in a social conversation.

The difference is that, in a high-maintenance situation, progress is less than likely to be made because it no longer is the high-maintenance person's goal. The high-maintenance employee is looking for attention, power, or some variation of these.

If the supervisor, manager, or executive provides this, she or he can expect...you guessed it...more visits from their new high-maintenance best friend because behavior that is reinforced tends to be repeated.

To put it succinctly, this does no one any good.

When I was first a supervisor, I attended several training classes in which I was advised to always listen to employees who worked with and for me. This has a nice ring to it and, with many employees, it is exactly the right way to go.

With a high-maintenance person, however, it simply adds fuel to the fire.

At this point, I feel compelled to repeat that most employees want to do a good job. It's just easy to get off track, particularly if the employee has signed on for a position because it was offered, because the money was great, or because their parents, best friend or spouse thought they should take it. In other words, they accepted without a true attachment to the contribution expected.

If the person who is the recipient of high-management behavior doesn't put a stop to it...escalation, and the associated costs, are probable.

A reasonable formula to correct high-maintenance behavior includes the following:

A definition of the situation, preferably using the term, "high-maintenance". This descriptor can be used gently and the point will still be made.

A restatement of the Vision/Mission/Goal and related expectations re:

> Profitability
> Effectiveness
> and
> Creativity.

A request for agreement regarding the expectations.

A *specific* comparison of current results compared to expectations.

A dialogue about the reasons for the expectations.

Reinforcement of the employee's value as a human, including acknowledgement that most humans want to perform well.

Reinforcement of the employee's value *(when she or he is performing well)*.

Explanation of the employee's high-maintenance behavior cost to the organization.

Request for performance change.

Mutual development of Groundrules for future performance.

Identification of assistance source(s).

Ramifications if high-maintenance behavior is not corrected.

SAMPLE SCRIPTS

With each of the following scripts, there are several pre-conversation considerations.

If the high-maintenance employee is one who comes and "parks" in your work area, go through the Physical/Mental/Emotional check, take a breath and begin.

If the high-maintenance employee is one who "catches" you outside the Men's or Ladies' Room, in the cafeteria or in the hall, go through the Physical/Mental/Emotional check, take a breath and ask if he or she has time for a brief conversation. If the answer is "Yes," invite them back to a suitable location. If he or she indicates this is not a good time for them, set up a time that is mutually convenient.

<u>NOTE:</u> If there is an inquiry regarding the purpose for meeting, you can truthfully respond, "There's a topic I've been wanting to review with you for awhile. Thanks for making the time."

If the high-maintenance employee is in another city, state, or country, check to see if either of you will (or can be) in the same location in the near future. If the answer is, "No," investigate teleconferencing facilities available with your organization or one of the many (relatively inexpensive) web-based conference services. Visual contact is important in this discussion. If the answer is "Yes," schedule your conversation for that timeframe.

Time Wasting

For this script, the employee is called Tom and the Employer is called Stan. The location is Stan's office. When Tom arrives, he is asked if he would like coffee/tea/water. In this case, Stan has a small round conference table and both men take a seat there.

Stan: "Tom, I've given a great deal of thought to this discussion because I consider it an important one."

Tom: "I'm not sure why you asked for this meeting."

Stan: "Well, I guess you could say it's a meeting to assess your satisfaction level."

Tom: "My satisfaction level with what?"

Stan: "Your position, the work you're assigned, your co-workers…you know, the whole picture."

Tom: "It's fine. Why do you ask? Are you asking everyone about this? I haven't heard anyone else mention it?"

Stan: "I'm asking because I have a concern and you are the only one with whom I'm having this discussion at this time.

Also, I want to tell you that, if my wife asks me how she looks and I say, 'Fine,' she doesn't consider my comment a ringing endorsement. And, to be honest, when I asked you about your level of satisfaction and you said, 'Fine,' I understood how she must feel."

Tom: "You know, it's good. No job is perfect."

Stan: "I'm betting that there are one or more areas in which you would like significant change... based on your behavior."

Tom: "Based on my behavior?"

Stan: "Yes. I might even classify it as "high-maintenance." To elaborate, I've noticed, in the last few staff meetings that you seem to take a less-than-positive approach to suggestions made by your peers. I've also noticed that, when the discussion is around a topic in which you have a strong interest, you are slow to close off the discussion."

Tom: "I'll try to be more positive. I wasn't aware... [*voice trails off*]..."

Stan: "Rather than just have you commit to making a change because of my observations, I'd like to understand why the situations I described might be occurring and...of equal importance... I'd very much like to take a look at their cost to the organization."

Tom: "Their cost to the organization?"

Stan: "That's right, Tom. When our organization hires or promotes someone, we hope to have extended an offer to someone who will, among other things, strive for maximum effectiveness and be very careful with our money."

Tom: "I've never exceeded my assigned budget."

Stan: "That's true. You haven't. On the other hand...well...let's just look at last Friday's meeting. I asked for suggestions regarding improvements to our customer delivery scheduling. After our brainstorming, you probably remember that we prioritized the items the group had come up with and then started a discussion around the possibility of their implementation."

Tom: "I remember that...clearly."

Stan: "Let me ask, and I want to do this gently, do you also remember that you argued against every item on the 'short list'?"

Tom: "I just wanted to get my thoughts out for consideration."

Stan: "And, while you were getting your thoughts out, did you happen to look around the table at the other meeting participants?"

Tom: *[...looking puzzled...]* "No. I don't remember doing that."

Stan: "If you had, Tom, I believe you would have noted that the others were rolling their eyes, shuffling papers, looking at their watches and checking e-mails on their PDAs. I'm not condoning their actions. And I do want to say I felt like doing the same thing. That's when I decided you and I needed to have this conversation."

Tom: "You wanted to talk with me because other people didn't like my ideas?"

Stan: "No. I want to talk with you because wasting others' time isn't effective, costs this organization money and, because of that, finding a better way to handle the situation is important.

I've made some rough calculations of the cost *[Stan looks down at his notes]* and it appears to me the portion of the meeting I've referred to probably cost the organization somewhere in the neighborhood of $1,100."

			Per Minute	
Attendee	Annual Salary	Hourly Salary	Salary	
Louis	$85,000.00	$40.87	$0.68	
JoAnne	$92,000.00	$44.23	$0.74	
Roger	$125,000.00	$60.10	$1.00	
Alice	$57,000	$27.40	$0.46	
Tom	$97,000.00	$46.63	$0.78	
Stan	$175,000.00	$84.13	$1.40	
				for every unnecessary minute of
			$5.06	discussion
			30	unnecessary minutes
			$151.68	
				7 group meetings the last 3 months
			$1,061.78	

STAN'S NOTES:

Tom: "Well, $1,100 isn't anything to blow off. And, given the dollars associated with our projects, it isn't earth shattering, either."

Stan: "That's true, Tom, unless you're using this behavior in the meetings you attend every day, probably 3 or 4 at the least, 5 days a week. If that's the case, the cost could be enormous. "
Both men sat silent for a few seconds. Then, Stan said, "Tom, until recently you have been a valued employee. When we hired you, one of the reasons we did so was the point you made in your interviews with myself and others about your desire to make a very positive contribution. When you came on board, your positive energy was admired by everyone who worked with you. I feel strongly that you are a good person and that we made a good hire. Will you help me understand

what has happened to that positive and effective approach?"

Tom: "I'm stunned that I might be detracting from my contribution by adding cost rather than supporting efficiency and that you think I've changed. I don't think I have, though I have noticed people responding differently to me lately. Let me think about this for a minute."

[Pause…]

Tom: "Honestly, Stan, I don't know what to say. I wasn't aware…"

Stan: "Tom, let's do this…let's agree that this behavior will stop. Can I rely on you for this?"

Tom: "Of course."

Stan: "To ensure this, is there a way I and others can signal you if it appears you've lapsed back into what I refer to as 'high-maintenance behavior'?"

Tom: "[smiling slightly] If you, or anyone, will just say something like, '…a bit high-maintenance today, are we?' I'll get the message."

Stan: "Get the message and curtail the behavior?"

Tom: "Yes. Absolutely."

Stan: "Tom, I'll use your suggestion and I'll offer it's use to others, too.

[Pause...]

I want this change to happen, Tom. You can make a very valuable contribution here and that's ex-actly what I want to see."

Tom: "That's what I want to do. That's why I wanted the position here in the first place."

Stan: "Great. Let's go forward then. If I can sup-port you with your efforts to change your high-maintenance behavior, please let me know."

Tom: "I will, Stan. And thank you for letting me know about this. In other organizations, people might not have been as thoughtful. I won't let you down."

Stan: "I'm counting on that."

NOTE: *It's amazingly easy for an employee to drift into high-maintenance behavior without realizing it. In Tom's case the direct feedback about his behavior's impact will probably be enough to turn those behaviors around.*

DEBATING

For this script, the employee is called Jan and the Employer is called Ross. The location is a small conference room. Ross has just explained a new assignment he is delegating to Jan.

Ross: "So, Jan, do you have any questions about this assignment?"

Jan: "I guess my first question is, why are you giving it to me? My schedule is already full."

Ross: "You're the only person in the department who has previous experience with a program like this."

Jan: "Well, yes, I know. Still, how is anyone else ever going to gain experience without an assignment like this?"

Ross: *"This situation is too serious to give to an inexperienced person. That's why I decided to give it to you, Jan."*

Jan: *"Well, I just don't know if I have the time..."*

Ross: *"Is there another project I can take from your assignments and give to one of your peers?"*

Jan: *"Oh no. I've already got something going on my other projects."*

Ross: *"There must be something you would be willing to part with."*

Jan: *"I've got the action plans mapped out. Why would you want to take them away now."*

Ross: *"Because the program I'm assigning you is of great importance and you have experience."*

Jan: *"How about Bob? He's a good project manager."*

Ross: *"I agree. Bob is a good project manager. However, he has no experience in this area."*

Jan: *"Well...I guess I can do it. I'll probably need a couple of comp days afterwards, though, because I'll have to put in some long hours."*

Ross: *"Jan, you know there's a freeze on compensatory time. We're trying to get a true handle on our staffing needs so we're holding everyone to regular hours and work weeks."*

Jan: *"But I can't get it done during regular hours. My plate is too full."*

Ross: *"As I said, I'll be happy to reassign one or two of your projects to free up your time for this one."*

Jan: *"But I'm already involved in them. I like them. I don't want to give them up. We don't have to tell anyone about the comp time."*

Ross: *"Come on, Jan. You know I don't work that way. Just make a decision about which projects you want me to give to others and you can get started on this."*

Jan: *"I just don't see why I have to be penalized because of my past work history."*

Ross: *"Penalized? Are you kidding? This project has great visibility. You can be a star if you perform well on this project."*

Jan: *"I think I always perform well. You've said so. Is there something you're not telling me?"*

Ross: [exasperated and looking at his watch] "Jan, the only thing I've not told you is how much I dread giving you a new assignment."

Jan: "Well, it certainly doesn't feel like you dread assigning me new projects."

Ross: "But, I do. It feels as though you become really 'high-maintenance' because it's always a debate. This conversation, for instance, has taken ¾ of an hour. If I cost that out…[Ross scribbles quickly on a notepad as he punches a calculator]…you just cost the company $65 I'm guessing we'll have three or four more of these debates each week for the next month until this project is done. That will come to… around $1,000. And you know what, Jan, that's about the amount I would have bonused you for the successful completion of the project we've been debating. I probably won't be bonusing you because I'm already doing so through lost time."

Jan: "It sounds like you're saying I'm inefficient and uncooperative."

Ross: "It feels, to me, as though you are uncooperative and these debates are inefficient. I mean, you're bright and have good experience…it's always just such a battle to talk with you."

Jan: "Ross, I'm stunned. I had no idea you felt this way."

Ross: *"I'm not the only one, Jan."*

Jan: *"Okay, before we go one step farther, let's talk about what I need to do to correct the perception that I'm hard to deal with. Can we do that?"*

Ross: *"Only if it doesn't turn into a debate…my budget can't take two hits in one day."*

Jan: *"No debate. Let's talk."*

Ross: *"Okay. And I want to say I'm actually relieved we're having this discussion. I really want you to do well here and I feel what I term 'your high-maintenance behavior' gets in your way."*

Jan: *"How long have you been feeling this way?"*

Ross: *"Almost since you got here. Remember the customer meeting with Bill Evans your first week on the job?"*

Jan: *"I do remember that. I thought it went well."*

Ross: *"Well, we got the order and that's good. What you don't know is that I got a call asking about your approach right after the meeting. The customer was actually worried that you were going to be hard to deal with."*

Jan: "Why didn't you tell me, Ross?"

Ross: "I thought it was just new job jitters. When it continued, I just refused to deal with it, I guess. You've probably noticed I don't like conflict."

Jan: "And I'm just the opposite. "

Ross: "I've certainly noticed that."

Jan: "I guess I grew up that way. My family fought like cats and dogs…over everything."

Ross: "Mine never fought…at least not publicly."

Jan: "We're products of our rearing."

Ross: "That's probably true and today may be a good time for both of us to 'sign on' for a behavior change…one that is more effective and less costly to the organization."

Jan: "I'd never thought of it that way, but we have both been costing the organization by not working this out."

Ross: "That's true. So, let's take an oath…"

Jan: "You're kidding, right?"

Ross: "Well…about the oath…not about the commitment. I'll make it. Will you?"

Jan: "I will. It actually feels good to me. I want to be recognized for good work."

Ross: "I think the change we're talking about will be a great help in that regard."

Jan: "Ross…"

Ross: "Yes…"

Jan: "If I 'fall off the wagon,' will you help me get back on?"

Ross: "You can count on it. That will be part of my learning curve. We'll help each other."

Real Life Scenarios

High Maintenance Employee Scenario #1

Tanya Brown literally raced from the parking lot to the building. Squeezing into an already crowded elevator, she burst out at the 3rd floor. Two second later, she was inside her office and reaching for the phone.

"Schedule changes," she muttered emphatically to herself! "I didn't need this today."

As Tanya spoke quickly into the phone, she sifted through a stack of folders looking for the report about which she must know everything in two hours. It was a big report, filling an equally big binder and decorated with yellow post-its

throughout marking points of special importance.

Beginning to both read and make notes, Tanya
didn't hear her office door open. When the staff
member said, "Tanya, do you have a minute?"
and sat down comfortably in one of the office's
guest chairs she felt mildly nauseous.

"Actually, Beth, I'm preparing for the big meeting at 1:00 p.m. and I need every second I can
squeeze out of this morning."

"Oh," Beth responded, "this won't take long. I
just wanted to ask about my performance evalu-
ation."

"That," thought Tanya, "is definitely a topic for
another day."

"Beth," she said, "I'd love to talk about this and I
really cannot do it now. Would Wednesday morning be convenient for you?"

Beth looked pouty. "The Employee Handbook
says we can ask for a discussion of our performance at any time," she whined.

"Any *reasonable* time, with *reasonable* notice,"
Tanya corrected mildly.

"I just want to make sure I'm doing everything the way you want it done," Beth implored.

"You're not," Tanya thought to herself…"and I'm going to have to get into this whether I have the time or not."

SCENARIO #1 QUESTIONS:

1. Have you ever had an experience like this?

2. How did you handle it?

3. What was Tanya's first mis-step?

4. What was yours?

5. What could Tanya have done?

6. What could you have done?

Check you answer with the answers to Questions 3 and 5 on page 61.

High Maintenance Employee Scenario #2

Bob Rogers relished the half-hour or so in the morning when he had his department all to himself and he used this time to do real "thought work." So much of his day required making snap decisions and switching tracks very quickly that he liked to address the most complicated issues during his "alone time."

This morning, Bob was looking for a report from the corporate legal staff when he inadvertently picked up the Compensatory Time Report for his employees. Beverly, his Admin., had set them neatly on his desk for him to approve. Absent-mindedly (his mind still on the search for the legal document), he thumbed through the cards.

Suddenly he stopped. Brian Tracy's notation reflected 10 hours of comp time the past week. Puzzled, Bob thought there must have been a mistake. After all, he mused, Brian was working on one of the largest projects in the department and the due date was coming up.

Uncomfortable with what he saw on the report, Bob continued his quest for the legal document… and he kept a sharp eye out for Brian's arrival. About five minutes later, he heard Brian's familiar laugh as he and another employee came through the double doors.

"Brian," Bob said, stepping into the hallway, "Can I visit with you for a minute?"

"Sure, Bob," Brian responded amiably and, as he walked into Bob's office, "What's up?"

"Well, I'm sure it's a mistake, but the Comp Time Report indicates you used 10 hours of comp time last week and—with your current project—I am sure that couldn't be accurate."

"Actually," Brian said, completely unfazed, "It is correct. I had done everything I could on the project so I just took off. I had some errands to run and needed to have my car serviced."

Bob could hardly believe his ears. "Explain what you mean by 'you had done everything you could on the project.' "

"Well," Brian began, "Accounting hasn't finished their reports for me and H.R. hasn't assigned the Intern I requested, and…"

"Whoa!" Bob stopped him. "Why am I only hearing about this now? Are we still on track for project completion?"

"It will probably come in a little later than projected. I would have been on target if everyone had just done their job. Since they didn't, I'm behind," Brian explained.

"Brian, I can't believe what I'm hearing. Why didn't you let me know or why didn't you talk with Accounting and H.R.?" Bob was flabbergasted!

"I sort of thought that would be your job," Brian said, looking uncomfortable.

"It's my job <u>and</u> your job. This is a team deliverable." Bob could feel his face getting red.

"Well…gee…I don't know what to say. The Project Guidebook says the manager will be responsible for follow-up…not the employees," Brian offered.

"Certainly the manager bears ultimate responsibility. It's just that, if you commit to an assignment and it derails, you have a responsibility to let the manager know so he or she can respond appropriately," Bob said evenly.

"I've never seen anything about employee re-sponsibilities—other than technical, of course—in the Project Guidebook," Brian persisted.

"Wait, Brian," Bob sat down and motioned for Brian to do the same. "Are you telling me you don't understand that, if a project we've accepted is failing, anyone and everyone has a responsi-bility to alert someone who can initiate correc-tive measures...that each of us—regardless of our role—has a responsibility for effectiveness, productivity and profitability?"

"I just go by the published rules, Bob. You've never said this to me before."

SCENARIO #2 QUESTIONS:

1. Have you ever had an experience like this?

2. How did you handle it?

3. What was Bob's first mis-step?

4. What was yours?

5. What could Bob have done?

6. What could you have done?

Check you answer with the answers to Questions 3 and 5 on page 62.

High Maintenance Employee Scenario #3

The Board Meeting was over. Meredith Jones kicked her shoes off under her desk and leaned her chair back. This had been a good one.

The new Board President had been complimentary about several things, not the least of which was the upcoming fundraiser.

Meredith was looking forward to this, too. A successful event would guarantee funding for two new services to local Seniors, something she had been working toward for three years. And it was going to happen. She felt good!

As she was basking in the glow of the meeting, Andie, the agency's Director of Development, stuck her head around the door. She had a troubled look on her face and asked, "Meredith, do you have a minute?"

Meredith looked up, smiled and said, "Of course."

Andie sat in the chair across from Meredith. "Houston, we have a problem," she began.

As Andie began talking, Meredith felt the quality of her day disappearing. What she was hearing was that the fund raiser for the new services was in jeopardy.

"...and I was so sure she would let us use her home..." Andie was saying as Meredith tuned back in.

"Andie, last week you told me this was a done deal," Meredith stated flatly.

"I know. I know. I thought it was," Andie replied, giving her head a disbelieving shake. "I still can't believe she won't do it."

Suddenly, Meredith recalled a similar conversation with Andie a year or so earlier when a scheduled event had to be rescheduled due to a location not having been secured. At the time, Meredith chalked it up to Andie's status as a new employee. "A new employee who came with excellent references and, also, who was highly recommended by her cousin, the person who is now the Board President," she thought to herself.

"Andie, how did this happen?" Meredith asked.

"Well…I spoke with the location's owner and she seemed to be on board. Now I find out she will be in Europe at the time of our fund raiser," Andie said with a shrug.

"Andie, I am concerned…on two fronts." Meredith paused.

"First, we don't have a site for the fundraiser that is looming on the horizon. Second, this is the second time a location you have assured me was secured…wasn't."

"I'm sure I'll be able to find another location," Andie said, still (in Meredith's opinion) appearing somewhat blasé.

"Please do that…quickly. And, as soon as we're past this crisis…and that's what it is, Andie, I want the two of us to have a conversation about expectations—both yours and mine, and the cost of crises to the agency." Meredith sincerely hoped the fear and disappointment she felt inside wasn't seeping into her comments.

"Okay," Andie replied and, for the first time, in Meredith's opinion, she looked concerned. "Do you think I should call Aunt Jill [the new Board President] for a recommendation?"

SCENARIO #2 QUESTIONS:

1. Have you ever had an experience like this?

2. How did you handle it?

3. What was Meredith's first mis-step?

4. What was yours?

5. What could have done?

6. What could you have done?

Check you answer with the answers to Questions 3 and 5 on page 63.

SCENARIO #1 SOLUTIONS:

What was Tanya's first mis-step?

Tanya's first "mis-step" was in not pleasantly stopping Beth from "parking" in her office.

What could Tanya have done?

Tanya could have stood up, looked Beth in the eye, stated that she, too, considered performance discussions important, apologized for not being able to speak with at that moment and set a time for the two of them to talk...making a note to include high-maintenance behaviors as one of the discussion topics.

SCENARIO #2 SOLUTIONS:

What was Bob's first mis-step?

Not establishing—and asking for commitment to--Groundrules regarding expectations, overall for the organization and specifically for the project.

What could Bob have done?

Actually, Bob "kept his cool" and that was effective. Together he and Brian can agree on next steps for this (and future) projects.

NOTE: Inclusion of other team/project team members for both input and commitment is definitely recommended.

SCENARIO #3 SOLUTIONS:

What was Meredith's first mis-step?

Not establishing Groundrules regarding expectations:

With Andie's aunt (the new Board President)
With Andie at the beginning of her employment
With Andie following the first location crisis

What could Meredith have done?

Obtained Andie's commitment regarding process and timeframe for new site selection following a "teaching review" of both.

Reinforced [very] tactfully that Andie reports to the Executive Director who reports to the Board.

NOTE: It would be very important for Meredith to have a discussion with the new Board President (Andie's aunt), emphasizing both Andie's skills and her areas for growth.

IN SUMMARY

The topic of High-Maintenance Employees is one that requires attention in today's workplace.

When doing so, it is important to remember:

1. Most high-maintenance employees want to do a good (maybe even great) job

   and

2. High-maintenance behavior is incredibly costly.

I've been told—and I've observed—that what gets measured gets handled. Measure and communicate high-maintenance costs and watch your productivity and profitability increase!

www.ingramcontent.com/pod-product-compliance
Lightning Source LLC
Chambersburg PA
CBHW022133170526
45157CB00004B/1867